Chaos to Success

Chaos to Success

INNOVATIVE STRATEGIES FOR CREATING CLARITY AND PROGRESS FOR COMPLEX PROJECTS

David Nimmo

ISBN-13: 9781505724097
ISBN-10: 1505724090
Library of Congress Control Number: 2015908133
CreateSpace Independent Publishing Platform
North Charleston, South Carolina

For my wife, Catherine

Contents

Acknowledgments

I wish to personally thank the following people who helped by inspiring me and guiding me as I created this book:

Catherine—my wife, most important collaborator, encourager, and constructive critic. We enjoy the roller-coaster ride of life's chaos together.

My daughters—Lettie, Katie, and Jemimah—the greatest sources of chaos and joy in my life. Without them, I would know only half as much as I do today about life.

My good friend, entrepreneur, and fellow cinema enthusiast Calvin for helping to keep me sane and for challenging my ideas through demonstrating what is possible when you commit to a vision and overcome the chaos to win.

Ari Galper and his team for their encouragement, guidance, and editorial input in making this book a reality.

All of my friends, professional and business colleagues, and past and present clients for sharing your knowledge, skills, and good humour with me and for keeping me grounded.

If you're trying to achieve, there will be roadblocks. I've had them; everybody has had them. But obstacles don't have to stop you. If you run into a wall, don't turn around and give up. Figure out how to climb it, go through it, or work around it.
—Michael Jordan

Introduction

You need this book. That's why I'm writing it for you.

I know you're really good at what you do—you have skills and experience I can only dream of. Maybe you're a program or project manager; an enterprise or solution architect; a change manager; or a unit or managing director, manager, or chief executive officer (CEO). Basically, you're someone who needs to get your organisation from where it is today to tomorrow's vision of performing at its peak.

But you're stuck.

You have deadlines to meet, progress to make, and people to bring along on the journey, and it's not happening. You're worried. In fact, the worries are starting to pile up, and you're wondering how you can make them go away. You're not sleeping very well, and facing work each day is becoming a challenge—and not in a good way.

Your progress reports need green lights, but they're currently yellow or red.

The people and teams who should be helping you get from A to B seem to want to take detours to every other letter in the alphabet. Your technology team is telling you things can't be done. Your business folks can't clearly tell you their problem and can barely define their vision for a solution. It's tough!

Sound familiar?

I know. I've been there. I've worked alongside program managers, project managers, strategists, architects, and directors—all tasked with spearheading change and all floundering at some point in the journey.

If you have that responsibility and you have reached that point (and I would be surprised if you haven't), then you are the person this book is written for.

Based on my experience of nearly twenty years supporting and advising change leaders (whatever their role title), I'll share with you stories and insights that will help you to break through whatever it is that is holding you back right now.

Let's get your project-, program-, or business-change initiative back on track so you can get back to driving the outcomes you want to achieve and so you don't lie awake at night wondering how you're going to push through.

I'll look forward to hearing your story of breaking through the chaos to achieve success!

To your success,

David Nimmo

Bonus Resources for Readers of *Chaos to Success*

As a bonus to readers of *Chaos to Success*, I've set up a special resources page on my NeoViz company website. Please check in there regularly for templates, tools, and resources I'll be adding to help speed you on your way to success!

www.neoviz.com.au/book-resources

Being stuck is a position few of us like. We want something new but cannot let go of the old— old ideas, beliefs, habits, even thoughts. We are out of contact with our own genius. Sometimes we know we are stuck; sometimes we don't. In both cases we have to do something.
—Rush Limbaugh

ROADBLOCK #1

Are You and Your Project Stuck?

The Roadblock

Sometimes you feel like you haven't made any meaningful progress in days, weeks, or maybe months. It's pretty frustrating, right? You didn't start out this way. You probably had every intention of making your mark—of putting your stamp on the business and leaving it a better, smoother-running, more profitable, and more enjoyable workplace than you found it.

When you've become stuck, that early optimism can start to seem like perhaps it was just naïveté. Now reality has set in, and that's just plain depressing!

Becoming stuck is a common experience. I've been there, and it's not fun. In fact, left unaddressed, over time the lack of progress and achievement can be downright soul destroying.

Where Does It Come From?

How does it get this way? Does it have to be this way?

Honestly, getting bogged down and stuck is simply the end result of a few simple forces acting against you, and they are forces that can be overcome.

The most basic force acting against you is resistance to change. People in general are resistant to change. People in groups multiply that resistance. Large organisations institutionalise the status quo and turn resistance into a virtue.

In response to significant resistance over time, a natural result is that you, the leader and instigator of change, become both despondent and exhausted, with little or no hope, energy, or motivation to move ahead. Instead of driving change, you settle for the status quo, for mediocrity, for productivity at a level of which you cannot be proud.

Tips for Busting Through

When you have been stuck for some time, whether it's days or months, there are a few simple things you can do to get that progress happening again (or perhaps for the first time).

1. Reflection

I cannot overstate the importance of reflection when you want to break through this roadblock. Overcoming any obstacle requires identification, definition, and acknowledgment of that obstacle (reflection). The more detailed definition you can give to this obstacle, the more concrete it becomes in your mind, and the better equipped you will be to recognise and face this enemy to your progress. Write down everything you can about this "stuck" roadblock, including how it makes you feel.

2. Envision Progress

Write down what progress would look like to you. Does it mean your team gaining new skills to become more productive? Does it mean making more sales or reducing costs through implementing more efficient processes? Whatever concrete milestones will define progress for you, write them down.

Change and leadership are first and foremost creative exercises: the creation of something new and better begins first in the mind and second in the physical world. So my encouragement is always to dream big and envision progress as specifically and clearly as you can. Then document your vision in words and pictures to make it concrete for yourself so you can communicate your objectives clearly to others.

At home, on my study wall, I have a number of charts and drawings visualizing my dreams and goals. I don't check in on them every day, but when I do, I am often amazed at how many I can check off as achieved, and what a great feeling that is.

3. Plan—Act—Measure—Celebrate—Repeat

Once you've reflected on the problem and have a clear picture in your head about what success looks like, then use this little process to create some forward momentum. Plan your next three steps, making sure you define how you will recognise when each step is "done" and successful. Write down these steps and measures to make them more concrete. Share them with an accountability partner if you find that helpful. Act to undertake the first step in your plan. Measure the success of that step. Celebrate the completion of that step—that could mean treating yourself to a nice lunch, a movie, your favourite chocolate, or whatever feels like a celebration to you—to reinforce your sense of positive momentum and progress. If you simply continue to repeat these steps, you'll find it won't be long before you can look back over your shoulder at the "stuck" roadblock miles behind you in the distance.

A Story

Phil had recently taken on a managing-director role in a poorly performing organisation, and he was struggling to make progress towards his own objectives and those of the stakeholders to whom he was accountable. Phil was stuck!

Phil was a very experienced and competent professional who was hamstrung in his new role due to an overload of complexity, in the form of multiple, conflicting operational (staffing, performance, client demands) and strategic (changing business models, changing competitive environment) issues. Phil had the skills to address and resolve each and every one of those issues but lacked a clear approach to create the order and space he required to allow him to prioritise and address the issues in a systematic way.

I met with Phil regularly over a number of weeks to collaborate on a range of approaches that would assist him to identify the information he needed to equip himself to make effective plans and decisions. Together, and working with his leadership team, we created a list of the various initiatives in progress around the organisation. We described each one and identified who was working on it and what stage it was at (planned, started, in progress, or complete).

Phil then identified and prioritised the top twenty initiatives that were important to him and his stakeholders. For those top twenty, we were then able to define next steps and deadlines, which would be tracked on a weekly basis.

The result of this work was that we achieved a significant reduction in Phil's anxiety and perceived lack of progress and control. Phil was better able to see and drive progress, steer and monitor his team's investment of resources, and therefore reduce wasted effort and focus on the changes and developments that would bring the biggest returns.

Phil reined in the chaos and created a clear and manageable plan to escape from being stuck and regain a sense of control over the organisation. That's an outcome worth fighting for!

For the past thirty-three years, I have looked in the mirror every morning and asked myself: "If today were the last day of my life, would I want to do what I am about to do today?" And whenever the answer has been no for too many days in a row, I know I need to change something.
—Steve Jobs

ROADBLOCK #2

Don't Know Why Change Isn't Happening?
There's a Formula for That

The Roadblock
You think you have all of the right ingredients in place, but you are still not achieving the progress you would like to see in your organisation. How do you figure out the root cause of this lack of progress, and how do you fix it?

Where Does It Come From?
The following formula, and other similar ones, can be very useful in helping you to pinpoint why change in your organisation is not going the way you need it to. It can identify one or more root causes for the lack of effective change. Each of the symptoms and its likely cause is set out here.

$$C_{hange} = (V_{ision} * T_{rust} * D_{issatisfaction} * F_{irst\ Steps}) / R_{esistance}[1]$$

---

[1] My own version of a formula popularized by Dannemiller, K. D., & Jacobs, R. W. (1992). *Changing the way organizations change: A revolution of common sense.* The Journal of Applied Behavioral Science, 28(4), 480-498 (that version was D x V x F > R). That was in turn an adaptation of an original formula created by Gleicher and published by Beckhard, R. (1975). *Strategies for large system change.* Sloan Management Review, 16(2), 43-55 (that version was C = (ABD) > X where C is change, A is the status quo dissatisfaction, B is a desired clear state, D is practical steps to the desired state, and X is the cost of the change. (References sourced from Wikipedia - https://en.wikipedia.org/wiki/Formula_for_change)

1. Resistance to Change

As I have stated in Roadblock #1, humans resist change. People get comfortable doing things a certain way in familiar surroundings. Even when people whine and moan about the way things are run, you'll notice that most people still stay exactly where they are, doing the same things they do. You might think they even secretly find comfort in the routine—and they do.

So when you come along with your shiny new approaches, projects, and ways of doing things, guess what? You pose a direct threat to their comfort and their status quo.

That's a mighty big hurdle to overcome, and there had better be something in it for the people who need to change, or you'll be dragging them along with you like a deadweight chained around your leg.

2. Missing Vision = Lack of Clear Common Direction and Sense of Purpose

Have you ever worked in an organisation where there is a vacuum where the vision and future direction should be? It's no fun. No one is sure what senior management is doing; a career starts to feel more like a job, and a job starts looking like an exercise in seat warming. No one gets excited about coming to work each day in an organisation like that.

Lack of vision leads to organisational and individual disorientation. In my experience, it is often more correct to talk about a lack of clearly defined, communicated, and commonly held vision. It doesn't matter how wondrous and inspiring the vision for the organisation might be if no one knows it or understands it. So to avoid or overcome this issue, make sure there is a clear direction and vision for your organisation, and make sure it is clearly and consistently communicated.

3. Lack of Trust = Cynicism

While lack of vision creates confusion, a clearly defined vision can be met with cynicism when individuals do not trust leadership espousing that vision.

Are you moving from an organisation that is heavily dependent on face-to-face client service to one where you expect 90 percent of client transactions to occur online? Sure, in your mind that might mean your team can participate in more "high-value" work, but initially all they may see is their old jobs disappearing and new role descriptions for which they are not equipped.

So, naturally they may be cynical, especially if they have been burned before.

4. Satisfaction with the Status Quo = No Clear Motivation to Change

Business-as-usual teams in particular need a reason to change. The old saying "better the devil you know" is highly relevant to this situation. While a beautiful vision of the future might have been painted, and the initial steps on the path are clear, without a reason to leave Munchkin Land, Dorothy might have been quite content to sit around and eat lollipops all day long. A fire has to be lit under people – what has sometimes been called a "burning platform" – I'll examine this further in the following pages.

5. No Clear First Steps = No Way to Move Ahead

Vision is great! Don't start a program of change without one.

Vision is like the picture painted of the Emerald City in *The Wizard of Oz*—a wonderful destination where all of your problems can be solved.

To get there, though, you need a Yellow Brick Road—your First Steps!

Starting a program of change without a clearly defined plan of how to commence is a recipe for disaster. What exactly is it you are going to do? How will you measure and report on your progress? How will you know when you have succeeded? What will your team be doing day to day?

Once you get momentum going you can make course corrections as necessary, but without a clear set of steps about how to commence and make early progress, you'll find it's easy to quickly dissipate enthusiasm, exhaust resources, and achieve failure. As with a map for a long journey or a method for a complex recipe, don't attempt to make change without a path for your team to follow, or you'll find yourself in a dead end before you know it.

A Story

Corporation X was attempting to implement a new enterprise-software system across a traditionally multi-siloed organisation. The CEO was effectively invisible

most of the time and did not set or maintain a clear direction beyond an impera-
tive to save money and deliver services more efficiently. There was nothing inher-
ently wrong with these reasonable, aspirational goals, but they were not helpful
in guiding the organisation in how to get there. These goals were not inspirational
in motivating the team or even useful in guiding the organisation to know how to
identify when it had achieved the desired outcomes. The chief information officer (CIO), in a similar manner, failed to provide clear parameters for success and,
more importantly, failed to empower others to confidently define and execute
on such goals. In the absence of clarity and empowerment, lower-level managers
were afraid to commit to a direction for fear they would make "wrong" decisions.

Over the course of months, the result was wasted opportunity, lack of progress towards an integrated system and organisation, and a repeat of the old siloed
organisation on the new information-technology (IT) platform. Wasted money and
squandered enthusiasm won out because leaders who should have had a structured
approach to guide their organisation and conquer chaos failed to act effectively.

Tips for Busting Through

How do we break through this barrier? Address each of the areas required to
achieve a healthy and vigorous environment for change.

1. Minimise Resistance to Change

The rest of the tips in this section seek to maximise the forces that allow you
and your team to overcome resistance. How much you need to build up those
forces, and how fast change will happen varies greatly depending on the scale
of the resistance involved, and its sources. If you can minimise resistance, then
you do not need to build up the positive forces so much to achieve the same
rate of change, or you can conserve resources and focus building your positive
forces to needlepoint accuracy through clearly understanding the nature of the
resistance.

Does the resistance to change stem from fear of job losses? Focus you efforts
on creating a vision of a more enjoyable workplace, with new and different
opportunities for those who embrace the change process.

Is there an apathetic acceptance and level of comfort with the status quo? Focus on drawing out pain points and amplifying dissatisfaction.

Seek to understand your enemy – Resistance – so you can target your efforts precisely.

2. Vision—Create Common Direction and a Sense of Purpose

I love working with a team where there is a clearly defined vision for the work we are doing. When the outcome is clearly defined and worthwhile, the team rallies behind it and is energized by it. As a project manager or consultant, my task becomes easier because the team members are self-motivated and take initiative to get us towards the goal.

There are many ways to come up with the vision, and it can depend on the style of the leader and the experience and composition of your team. There's no right or wrong way to come up with the vision, as long as it is clear, worthwhile, and the team is on board with it.

3. Trust—Overcoming Cynicism

People are naturally cautious about change, especially where it is being led by a new unknown leader (or one who does not have a good track record). Trust depends on building your credibility with the team and the business; demonstrating consistency and reliability; building intimacy with the team (actively listening to their concerns, getting to know them better in social settings) and minimising any suggestion of self-interest on your part as a leader. I deal with Trust and Cynicism further in the next chapter.

4. No Clear Motivation to Change – Draw Out and Amplify Dissatisfaction

Steve Jobs had mastered the art of creating dissatisfaction. If you haven't heard the story of how he finally convinced the president of Pepsi-Cola division of PepsiCo, John Scully, to join Apple, it is a lesson in honing in on and amplifying dissatisfaction – even if it only exists in microscopic quantities. To jump to the end of the story, after many attempts to badger, cajole, coax and entice Scully to join Apple, Jobs issued him with this challenge: "Do you want to spend the rest of your life selling sugared water, or do you want a chance to change the world?"[2]

Wow! Knock-out punch! Scully joined Apple soon after.

This challenge pretty much embodied the key components of effective change – particularly the calling out and amplification of dissatisfaction (*Do you want to spend the rest of your life selling sugared water?*), painting of a vision (*Do you want a chance to change the world?*), and clear first steps (join Apple). This creates what I referred to earlier as a "burning platform" – basically, Jobs created a situation where he lit a fire under Scully. If Scully stayed where he was, he risked missing an opportunity to do something important, and would be marooned on a platform which Jobs had painted as ultimately meaningless and unfulfilling. How could Scully say no?

You might not be Steve Jobs, and your team might not be selling sugar water, but you can work with them to identify and call out their points of pain and dissatisfaction, and pair it with a vision for a better future, and steps to get there, to help them move forward.

5. No Way to Move Ahead—Create Clear First Steps

When it comes to plans to start change, I like to approach them "wide first, then deep." What I mean is, start at the vision level: "I want to go from all face-to-face customer service today to conducting 80 percent of our interactions online within two years."

Okay, so that's a start.

What I might do then is take it down one more level via the "wide" approach:

1. In the first six months, we will establish an online shopping cart and checkout for our products.
2. In the following six months, we will promote the online shopping option through social media and promotions.

---

2   Isaacson, Walter. *Steve Jobs*. Simon & Schuster, 2011

3. In the third six-month period, we will optimise performance of the online store and begin redeployment of staff from in-store to online customer-service roles.

4. In the final six-month period, we will finalise closure of uneconomical branches and upgrade fit-out and service levels at flagship branches.

Using that level of action planning, I have a framework to guide my approach with senior management and build out my more detailed plan for each six-month period.

I would continue to drill down within each six-month period until I had a detailed month-to-month plan, with all actions, objectives, and required resources detailed. My emphasis is always on the immediate month ahead – there is always a new set of "First Steps" there for the team to grasp onto and to action. The plan will continue to change and evolve over the life of the project, but at least I now have some "rails" to run on.

Life is not an easy matter...You cannot live through it without falling into frustration and cynicism unless you have before you a great idea which raises you above personal misery, above weakness, above all kinds of perfidy and baseness.
—Leon Trotsky

ROADBLOCK #3

Is Your Team Cynical about Change? How You Can Fix This

The Roadblock

Have you ever started work with a team on a project that management was very excited about, but where the business and project teams look as excited as the cast of Michael Jackson's *Thriller* film clip? (For those too young to remember, the characters were all zombies.)

Where Does It Come From?

It is likely that the team has change exhaustion—a mixture of cynicism and plain old tiredness resulting from too many consecutive change programs that have pushed them too hard, with too few positive results.

The cause is usually a result of management overpromising and underdelivering on consecutive projects, while each time asking for the team to put in the effort and the extra hours to make it all happen.

When the results don't materialise, when the incentives aren't forthcoming, or when management loses interest and cancels the project, the team is effectively being inoculated against future change programs.

So I guess you're going to be the new most popular person in the group?

Tips for Busting Through

This is a very negative environment and takes extra effort and initiative to break through. What you need to do is repair what has become a dysfunctional and untrusting environment and rebuild that trust.

1. Ensure You Have Secured Necessary Backing

Before you begin, it is critical, as early as possible, to ensure for yourself that you are indeed empowered and resourced to build that trust. If you are not assured of management support and resourcing, then you will have little chance of rebuilding a culture of progress, change, and success.

How you measure this backing can be specific to your particular organisation. In medium to large organisations, this often means ensuring that you have a signed-off and funded business case and that you have established sponsorship and governance structures with suitably senior stakeholders on board. At the other end of the scale, it could be as simple as an e-mail confirmation from your boss in response to an e-mail outline of your proposal.

I recommend always getting something in writing, though, because it can avoid a lot of confusion and pain later on if perhaps someone forgets that he or she had made a commitment to your initiative.

So whatever gives you the guaranteed initial and ongoing support you need, make sure you get it!

2. Build Trust

If you are assured of the necessary support, then you will need to immediately work on rebuilding trust wherever it is lacking in the business and project teams.

Initially this might involve a lot of listening. A suggestion is to ask people to write down five things they think have been done wrong with initiatives in the past and five things they would like to see happen in future initiatives, and to bring those things to a meeting where the objective is to hear them out and clear the air prior to commencing your new initiative.

As a sign of good faith, commit to three to five of the changes the team members want to see made, and ask them to keep you accountable.

3. Communicate

Set up a regular weekly or even daily forum where the team can communicate with you.

Set short-term achievable goals, and start setting them, tracking them, and celebrating them as a way of rebuilding trust and momentum.

You can't fix broken trust overnight, but with consistent behaviour and progress, you can dramatically improve the situation over time.

Yesterday we obeyed kings and bent our necks before emperors. But today we kneel only to truth, follow only beauty, and obey only love.
—Khalil Gibran

ROADBLOCK #4

If I'm Leading, Why Isn't Anyone Following?

The Roadblock

You're all set to make a difference, to exceed your clients' expectations, to deliver on time and on budget, and to the required level of quality. To make it happen, you need a high-performing team who will work with you and a group of businesspeople who are excited about adopting the amazing changes your team will bring.

But what are you presented with? More often than not, what you actually find is cynicism and change exhaustion in both your team and in the larger business. Let's assume you've taken steps to rebuild trust (see Roadblock #3). Now, how do you get the team working with you to achieve the outcomes you are aiming for?

Where Does It Come From?

If you look at children, you realise people are not born cynical. It takes years of opposition, politicking, stolen recognition, and lack of reward to create the type of deeply ingrained cynicism you will find in many individuals and teams in workplaces today.

Your project team has been on one too many "long marches" without a clear, meaningful outcome. Your clients and business stakeholders have been made promises in the past that have failed to deliver or live up to expectations. No wonder they are a little skeptical of the project and your vision of how things could be (despite your energy and enthusiasm!).

Tips for Busting Through

This roadblock can be overcome in increments. To build up ongoing cycles of success, try to keep the cycle of steps below to short time periods—as short as four weeks, but no longer than three months.

1. Prioritise

Work with the business to collaboratively determine the highest-priority business objectives that your team can consider delivering in a four- to six-week period.

It's invaluable to involve as many of the team as possible in this activity, as it builds firsthand understanding of business priorities for the team and provides an opportunity to create clarity and understanding that is very difficult to achieve any other way. It is an interactive process; questions from your team to the business may also help the business to understand subtle complexities in their own requirements that might not otherwise have been apparent.

There are many different approaches to this prioritization activity. I like to have all participants undertake some prework before the meeting. For the business representatives, this means independently prioritising each requirement and bringing that list along to the meeting (setting a prioritization approach helps— e.g., you can nominate only twenty priority items and scale them from one to twenty, using each value once, with one as the highest priority). For the change- delivery team, that means reading through the list and coming along with any questions or clarifications they might have.

In the meeting, each business representative (whether one person or a dozen people) should write out each requirement and the priority he or she has assigned it on a sticky note. The facilitator can then ask each businessperson to place each priority requirement on the wall, grouping sticky notes for the same requirement together. Once they're all up, the facilitator can tally the priorities for each item and rearrange them on the wall in order. The entire group can then review this and have discussion to determine an agreed priority order on the items.

This is only one approach, but in my experience, it can be a very useful one to encourage business decision making and building of understanding.

2. Confirm Priority with Stakeholders

Agree with the stakeholders that delivering those items will provide significant value to the business. Have the business representatives state in their own terms what that value will be, and why that is of high value to them.

If you have used the prioritization approach outlined above, you might already have a good understanding of what the business value is of the priority items. However, it is worth explicitly restating and documenting it for each priority item to maintain clarity about the purpose and rationale behind delivery of a particular feature or change.

An example for a change to an online-banking application for personal-banking customers might be as follows:

Change: Provide a clear confirmation to a user when a transaction has been successfully completed.
Business Value: Reduce complaints and inquiries to call centre from customers who are uncertain about whether transactions have been successfully completed.

Once business value and agreed priority have been confirmed, it is time for your delivery team to review their capacity to deliver the required changes within any defined resource, time frame, and quality constraints.

3. Confirm Team Capacity and Understanding

Confirm with your team that they understand the requested content, the expected outcomes, and the business value those outcomes will deliver. Confirm with your team what they are confident that they can deliver from the prioritised list in the agreed time frame.

This discussion can be undertaken as part of a separate meeting, with the outcome and any clarification questions taken back to another meeting with stakeholders.

One fun and effective way to confirm team understanding and capacity to deliver is to work through an estimating approach known as "planning poker." In this activity, each member of your team is provided with a set of planning poker cards. Each of the priority requirements is worked through in turn, explained, and a chance for clarifying questions allowed. Once you are confident the team has a good understanding of the requirement, each person selects a card representing the level of effort involved in delivery of that requirement, feature, or change.

Once all are ready, the cards are flipped over to reveal their selection. If all cards are the same, you are done—just record the value. If there is variation, facilitate discussion in the team and potentially redraw. After two or three draws on a requirement, the facilitator may, with the team's agreement, settle on a majority or agreed value.

While achieving an estimated value for each requirement is important, building the team's understanding of considerations for delivery of each item is also highly valuable.

Once values are settled on for each item, the team should review time, resource, and quality constraints and determine what portion of the prioritised requirements they can confidently deliver within those constraints.

4. Commit

In a follow-up meeting with business stakeholders, the delivery team will make a commitment to the business to deliver on the agreed objectives in the time frame. If for any reason the business is unhappy with where the delivery team "drew the line" in step three, the business may consider renegotiating the priorities or the time frame until both the business and the team have something they are all happy with as the scope for the particular piece of work.

5. Lead

Lead the team in delivering on that commitment and in helping them to overcome any obstacles. Depending on the approach you are using to manage the team and their work, your role may differ. What never changes, though, is that your role is to do everything in your power to set up ideal conditions for the team to succeed. Keep distractions away from them, make sure they have the resources they need, and keep the coffee coming!

6. Demonstrate Business Value Delivered

Demonstrate the value of the delivered commitment to your business client. Ideally, get your delivery team to lead this demonstration—after all, they delivered the outcome.

Demonstrate what was completed and how it meets the objectives the business defined up front.

Ensure the business acknowledges that the commitment you and your team made has been met. (If you've done your job right, this is not likely to require any coaxing on your part.)

7. Celebrate Success

Celebrate with your business client and your team, recognising the effort, the outcome delivered, *and* the trust built through your successfully keeping your commitment.

8. Onward to More Success!

Repeat steps one through seven until the job is done, and enjoy the sense of achievement along the way!

Building Leadership and Momentum

The main goal here is to establish communication and build trust step by step and cycle by cycle. Each successful cycle underlines a new level of trust and achievement, which will help you to overcome cynicism and burnout. That's why each cycle is kept nice and short, because each new cycle represents a new opportunity to build communication, trust, and momentum.

Instead of a manager whom your team begrudgingly obeys, you become the leader who lays the foundations and establishes the process for realising achievement and delivering success. As you demonstrate enthusiasm, optimism, and competence, your team can't help but develop trust in you and enthusiasm for the work at hand.

I can't tell you how many times I've seen these steps totally transform the way teams interact within themselves and with their business clients. Give it a try, and let me know how you do!

To err is human, but to really foul things up requires a computer.
—Bill Vaughan